Boomerangs in the Living Room

Boomerangs in the Living Room

poems

Rex Wilder

RED HEN PRESS | *Pasadena, CA*

Boomerangs in the Living Room

Book design and layout by Jaimie Evans

Library of Congress Cataloging-in-Publication Data
Wilder, Rex.
[Poems. Selections]
Boomerangs in the living room : poems / Rex Wilder.—First edition.
pages cm
ISBN 978-1-59709-269-2 (alk. paper)
I. Title.
PS3623.I539B66 2013
811'.6—dc23
2012039100

The Los Angeles County Arts Commission, the National Endowment for the Arts, the City of Pasadena Cultural Affairs Division, Sony Pictures Entertainment, the Los Angeles Department of Cultural Affairs, and the Dwight Stuart Youth Fund partially support Red Hen Press.

First Edition
Published by Red Hen Press
www.redhen.org

Acknowledgments

Several poems in this book, some in earlier versions or under different titles, appeared in the following publications:

The Antioch Review, "Forced)," "Pigeon)," "Were)," "Wilder)"; *Beloit Poetry Journal*, "On the Eve of the End"; *The New Republic*, "Found)"; and *Poetry*, "Near Affair."

Deepest thanks to: my spirit's life-companion, Jessica Hornik Evans; Kate Gale, for believing my second book could be a butterfly; Mark Cull and Jaimie Evans for dressing up the insect, along with Red Hen's Finest—Ashley Ellis, Gabriela Morales, Alysha Owen, Billy Goldstein, and Chris Konish; Alice Quinn, who caught the boomerang and ran with it; Andrew Filippone, for his sensitive appreciations of early boomerangs, which made subsequent forays more ambitious; Richard Wilbur, for his beautiful changes; my parents, Judy and Bernard Briskin, for their loving support, presence, and embrace, and Jack and Ann Marie Wilder, for their tropical cheerleading and triggering island; Angela, for her gracious literary salons, the *belle époque* she brought to Los Angeles on behalf of my dream and Red Hen's; Maha Yoga, for breath itself; Fred Miggins, for his goodness; and my dear friend Heather Neill, for the cover of this book by which I would prefer it be judged.

For Madeline, Simon, and Oliver,
all at once

Table of Contents

II.

III. Boomerangs

Author's Note

A new form, the boomerang, makes its debut in sections I and III of this book. As first conceived, it was rather a blunt instrument with only two real requirements: 1) that the first word or sound rhyme with the last; and 2) that it all fit on a single line in a readable typeface. Fortunately for the form's viability, the poet Richard Wilbur found himself beneath an autumn brainstorm. As he recounted to me,

> I used to throw boomerangs, years ago, and I remember that a thrown boomerang has three phases: it flies to first base (as it were), then travels over to third and rises, then swoops home. Rather like
>
> *How*
> *to put food on the table,*
> the cleaver asked
> the cow.

Anyone who has smiled through Wilbur's work, especially his poems for children, should not be surprised at the sophisticated sense of play that he has now lent to my own.

I hope you enjoy reading the boomerangs as much as I—with the master's hand guiding mine—enjoyed throwing them.

I

Boomerangs

UNDER)

Under ten,
they're still asking questions;
ten, it's over, the automatic
wonder.

Who)

Who
doesn't try to keep the hunter
happy? It's easy meat
at the zoo.

Late

Late check-out:
three hours for only thirty dollars.
A cheap mini-cheat
of fate.

Bruised}

Bruised
blue flames light spring:
this is how crocuses
are used.

And)

And George
is not *gorgeous, which is*
why I'm holding his
hand.

HERETICAL)

Heretical
tree-magnolias ignore the man,
their perfume
theoretical.

Discretionary}

Discretionary joy!
Deep brown dead grass does not dampen
the man's mowing
session.

Drops

Drops
of rain lay out their yoga
mats—and my pain
stops.

Views

Views
have no close relatives, only jealous
neighbors and a whorish
muse.

Hours

Hours, gone,
come! I have spent my life
trying to reattach
cut flowers.

Weird)

Weird
white flies buzz the old hibiscus'
face, ghosting
a beard.

Love

Love breaks
against dawn's shore until
no bed is wide
enough.

CAROUSEL)

Carousel!
Happened on. But
no one to
tell.

OLD

Old
people steady parents in temple;
they still do what
they're told.

CRÊPE)

Crêpe paper
hats at the alley party take me back
to my vampire days
in Dieppe.

Rungs)

Rungs of
this quiet's ladder wait for climbing
breath, collapsing
lungs.

PARK)

Park on
a bench: watch the ranger Distance
collect the dog’s
bark.

STORIES

Stories
told make you old, they
say, the morning
glories.

Glass

Glass
bottom tickling the kelp is glass
top to the dreamy
bass.

WAITING

Waiting
for a humpback to leap—
the sun and a sailboat
baiting.

Found

Found:
Home from the beach, an argument
we thought the surf
had drowned.

Surf)

Surf
is high, not modesty: her shirt says
True Beauty Is Within but it rises
to the surface.

Here's)

Here's
a forest at the farmers' market:
a tidy stand of asparagus
spears.

Sex)

Sex,
ours at least, is flipping cars and
climbing, unhurt, from
the wrecks.

Clueless

Clueless
tree-thoughts gain confidence—
lining up along my brain's
avenue.

PIGEON)

Pigeon,
poor pigeon, trying to kill
himself by jumping off
the bridge.

Embassy)

Embassy
flags flag; the wind blows
right through
them.

WILDER}

Wilder,
Rex. Mature poet (tweak
of nature). Man-
child.

Paraphrase}

"Paraphrase"
(of all words) runs off like a cat;
doesn't return for
four days.

Beds)

Beds,
pillows—religions? Tithe
our bodies' prayers
and tired heads.

Forced

Forced on her
like a pickle by Sandwich Sam (not
his name): leaky promises.
Divorced.

II

I Love the Poetry of the Old

I love the poetry of the old,
Strand, Yeats, Meredith, Lowell,
Even Keats if you count
The hundred years he lived in twenty-five.

In a sense it is English made young
Again, the years few again;
The codgers, if they can last long
Enough, are writing for their lives.

Beverly Theatre

I come from a family of forgetters, at least
That's how I remember it, who count on clues
To keep the past intact.
                                        So when I found
The carpeted walls, vaulted ceiling
And iridescent chandeliers of that street's last
Remembered childhood landmark gone,
A magnificent movie house spread like eraser dust
Behind a cordon beside the deli,
It was a small arcing blow, like static electricity
Generated by the heart, and my son
Saw the loss register on my face.
He leaned his shoulder against my forearm,
Suddenly but lightly, the way a boy his age might,
Close to perfection, adjust a stack of blocks.
"They're tearing down all your memories, Dad,"
He said, taking my side against all progress.

Star Soldiers

Jew-meat,
Cossack-prey, shtetl-girl (Grandma?)
presses her ruddy
new-

born
into silence's service. Against her breast,
centuries, winters.
Warn

Teresa's
neighbor! Bury everything but the boy
whom my father
replaces.

Hard to Say

"Tell me, is the more-or-less moth facing
  Up, gazing at night sky through vines,
Or down, to the sidewalk snails are lacing
  With their aimless trails and artless designs?
Lit from beneath or above by the horizontal
  Desk light, is it basking,
Stiller than a girl by a pool who wants all
  The sun to herself, asking
Nothing of the window other than purchase?
  Is it the picture of mental hurt or health,
Balanced gamely between the desire to chase
  Annihilating heat and the wealth
Of knowledge explaining the vanity therein?"

I was staring at the glass, past my face
And a furred reflection of the kitchen,
Before this ambiguity landed like a shred of lace
Blown from some dreamy venue
And I will be longing still in its ghostly wake,
Loving false and loyal to true—
Torn in two for wholeness' sake.

Amphibia

We crawl onto land every day,
Though the air isn't right
And the light refuses to waver.
Our wake, the water,
We call this longing Dance.
Oh the grace of that woman
Climbing the stairs!
Take me to her lily pad!
At work, we bury
The future; home, we honor
The dead. Our aim is true,
As it always has been.
We crawl onto land every day.

Corpus

Souvenir of my mother's time and father's place,
I'm a snow globe now on nobody's shelf;
Mom and Dad have left me to my self,
And the mirror, and two bodies' face.

Fire Ant

By my own rules
Do I measure,
My own jewels
Do I treasure.

I find my peace
Among the galaxies:
When I exclude,
I find my magnitude.

I am a fire ant.
I am ignorant,
Primitive, brass,
An insect king:

I do the electing.
I'm the picture of languor
Beneath your
Magnifying glass.

The Six O'Clock

In a class of seventy, I was the only one blinded:

The low sun poured through two small windows,

As if itself relaxing in corpse or savasana pose,

While we unwound and were hardly winded.

All were wide-eyed except for me. Not that I minded

Serving as shield and decoy for rows and rows

Of devotees. For a while, I was the setting

Sun's pet; I gave as much light as I was getting.

The Downpour

A rain unprecedented in June,
A monsoon, really,
Shakes me from sleep and bed and blows me to the window
And a view of the broken water main
Pouring freedom into the starry sky.
A woman once told me a lie like this,
Turning everything upside down
But doing nothing to cut the purity of my habit.
You can't start a sentence over
When you get to the punctuation.

Wisconsin Avenue, Georgetown

It's the graceful bodies we won't let go of,
The historic landmarks we protect.
The stores themselves are shallow souls that love
Us for our money and do not remember the architect.

'With the sun midway'

With the sun midway
Across the heavens on a summer's day
  At Vezin and pleasure
  Craft taking their leisure
A little too seriously—not even the parasailer wavers—
Forgive me if I say
    The lighting does no one any favors
    With its blunt and aimless beat
That makes us look artificially incomplete
And insanely same.
  Shadows seem halfhearted in their claim.
  Not even the two rock
Islands make the short list of the scenically elite
    At twelve or one o'clock.
    To love now would be to ignore
What's inside and what's in store.

Cut Memories

I take my memories for the short
Term, like cut flowers to be
Enjoyed for three or four days,
While still fresh, while not
Too receded, and before they become
Brown at the edges, and the voices
Change, and the hair
Assumes the color of the hour,
And the building where
The memory took place is torn down.
I like my memories before
The story of their disappearance
Gets old, when you can
Still inhale them off your pillow.

Grandpresents

Languorous in the semi-shade of the pear,
A canopy of blossoms crowding leaves
At least five seasons old, grandparents dare
Grandchildren to shoot, as each cleaves
To the love of basketball, or any game
Or gambit that brings loved ones home.

Time glows in dunks, banks, fallaways,
Swishes, no-look passes and alley-oops,
And, in the fans' hourglass, *thattaboys*
And voluble cheers extend the boys' hoops
At least an hour. Only the assimilated
Parrots in the silk tree see the day repeated.

The Second Floor

After nearly a year of hearing
  false rain play while we lay,
Eyes closed and posing for
  a blissful death—the real thing:
Nature's paean to restraint,
  the always measured display
Of sound at its shallowest,
  as Heaven and Earth sing.

So much was make-believe
  in that studio where we practiced
Eastern thinking above
  an Italian bistro in West L.A.
That this shred of authenticity
  was welcome artifice:
The perspiration of perfection,
  God trying, a roundelay.

Even the instructor seemed
  to appreciate the opportunity;
He turned off the expensive
  sound system and steered

His savasana patter to the end
of the drought. Our pretty
Bodies were an echo of the rain
drops, as we disappeared.

Echo, Echo!

Today, late
May, late me.
Romance
Streams, runnels
Of desire driving

Our sainted
Chaparral
Insane. I too
Was green once
And will be again.

Parity Island

Garibaldi, encelia, casino, cove,
Kelp-bed, Catalina cherry, blue—
When every noun around you
Achieves synonym status with love,
There's nowhere deeper to dive
Than the shallows they sell to the tourists
Or more healing than the salve
Of Here, where nothing persists.

Polynesiac

Sink, I said, trying
To submerge myself
A human's height
Beneath the surface;
Managed a moment,
Achieving parity
With the parrotfish,
Who let me gawk,
As if this turquoise
Room were the stage
Of a gentlemen's
Club. Breathless,
I turned a shade of
Blue myself, or so
The pretty panic felt.
Then once again
The dry world had
My back, and I
Floated like the corpse
Of ambition, shot
Down from shallow
Heaven. *We never*
Quite belong because
We always nearly

Belong: this, the Zen
Of the denizens
Of the deep. Sink,
I said, at ease
Again, after clearing
Water and air from
My snorkel. And
Down I went, another
Forty times at least,
Relentless dissenter,
To meet my
Uncomfortable fate.

In Danger, The Shallows

He's bold, or dead:
those are my first two guesses.
He resists or doesn't resist
my advances,
That's for sure, like a skin of ice,
or the bucket of a marriage.
What do you expect,
at my age—
That I would let anything
so blatant as love
Languish there?
He has the bearing of a lodge,
Somehow, though he is only
a monk seal,
Rare or rarer. For the first time
in my life, there is nowhere to fall.
He lifts his simian head
and caresses the spray;
Whiskers paddle his funny face.
"Nothing," I say.

Regnium Magnus

The gods are forbidden the bodies of mortals,
With a single exception: When pain and oblivion

Combine to cloak the union.
Hence Regnium, invisible in full sunlight

On the sidewalk beside the school.
Regnium could not wash the love off his hands

While the woman—a mother? a teacher?—
Whose bloody head he cradled

As her seizure settled knew nothing of his desire
But the dark mirror of it that caressed

Her awake. When paramedics arrived
They thought the panic in her shoulders

And whipping neck was another tremor
And worked to secure her with frayed

Straps and nerves, but she had come to:
Was looking desperately for any sign of him.

Roxboro Circle

for Madeline

The house you were raised in,
The home you amazed in
Was built to last forever,
Until you returned with a lover
Or a child of your own.
The three gas lamps alone,
Survivors of the Civil War,
Shone into the future, far
Beyond our neighborhood's
Circumscribing woods.
The home, I hear, was razed in
Haste a year ago or more
Along with the circular
Block itself: the spokes
Of lined trees and walks
And the round park at the center
That was our main square.

After a Blue Jay Falls through the Light and Disappears

I'm not alone or
even close when I return to the shore
at five and wait
for the sun to differentiate
Jeffreys from Ponderosas. It's always autumn at this hour,
when we discover who we are
courtesy of the most impersonal power.

Big Bear Lake

Jacaranda Squared

After night left us this unremarkable dawn,
Desaturated, odorless, our voluble son,

Mute now like something valuable, cached
Himself into a taxi, which rushed

Away, complicit. I remained on the side-
Walk with a piece of quiet, and stood

Awkwardly, as if I had just been handed
A heavy package or, Hemingway-lite, landed

A heavy fish. Two shuffling crows
Found me sane enough and allowed me to cross

Their path. I joined them, as at a *frites* stand.
"And what brings you *to the Land*

Of Dour Flowers?" the first one ventured,
Pecking at the translucent purple bells absurd-

Ly. *"Can't eat 'em, can't eat without 'em,"*
Opined the second on the same theme.

"My son is fourteen," I explained, as if
That said it. And should have; but a crow's life

Has different mile markers. I placed the ache
For them: *"His youth is dying of old age.*

*"The toy worshipper and daddy's boy, the humane
Snail- and spider-saver cannot take the pain."*

An SUV bearing down like truth Tased
Us off the philosophical avenue and erased

Its own intimidation before we knew
What didn't hit us. The lawn, Fitzgerald-blue,

Felt adult. *"You don't see the point
Of things until they're right under your feet."*

These the sage last words of the crows.
I picked sticky blooms from between my toes.

Porridge Day

At home among the fixed
And finished, I find inclusive
A questionable virtue and mixed
Ingredients impossible to love

Anymore. Oh uniqueness, where did
The cinnamon go? I can hard-
Ly taste it in this sauce. I died
Once when I lost myself in a crowd.

Doug Ritter's Great Man Theory

The acacia stands out from the dull live
Oaks and scraggly walnuts like a dictator
On a balcony, a ridiculously impressive
Hue doing a number on me, the spectator
And commuter. We the cynics worry
Too much about the distributors of glory,
Even as we bask in it, and try to matter.

On the Eve of the End

On the eve of The End,
  I open my rented curtains and let lightlessness seek,
In the glossy surfaces, like a first-time burglar,
    restitution, and easier ways out.

On the eve of The End,
  I dive beneath a breaking wave as clear as this vodka
And come up among splashing girls
    as drunk as I am, but on something purer.

On the eve of The End,
  the wind crams like soccer match hooligans through the gap
In the window jamb. *When something empties*
    into something, the memory of something remains.

On the eve of The End,
  a student sets himself on fire to make a point.
If he survives, he will no longer be welcome at the café
    where he came up with the idea.

On the eve of The End,
  the Woman of the World shrieks, the hotel-towel falls,
And the hemispheres of her breasts describe
    two perfect sunrises in a row.

To a Mermaid

The missionary fog would have all land sea,
And me a fish, or merman, and every tree
Salted and buffeted by current. Her grey grace
Sways me, admittedly, and some days,
I lean toward the ocean and half-convert,
Feeling foreign in the air, and flirt
With the idea of making a life in the ocean.
If only you were here to second the motion.

The Jungle Ride

  In line for the big ride, I was *his* ride.
He wrapped his arms around
  My waist, stood on my feet and hid
His face against me, riding backward
Blind. I saw it all over his head—
  The fake ruins, the spring-break crowd,
And my smile was Nile-wide.
Not until now, to my shame, a decade
  Later, do I wonder what *his* face said.

Villainelle

There's been a mistake. You're free to go. Be well.
Return to the world of light, see your hands again.
Vary your exit times. Avoid the rush from hell.

Turns out the plaintiffs had your evil spell
Coming. Your crime covered theirs; sin cleanses sin.
There's been a mistake. You're free to go. Be well.

There's bound to be a backup; security personnel
Are undertrained and emotional to a man.
Vary your exit times. Avoid the rush. Hell,

I'm choked up myself. I like you. You're real.
It hasn't been so bad, has it? Always a fire to fan,
At least. You're free to go. Be well,

My friends. Think of us here where first you fell,
Murder-fresh and cradling your weapon.
Vary your exit times. Avoid the rush from hell.

Remember the beauty in the soft swell
Of a wrong's grave; virtue has its day in the sun.
It's not a mistake. You're free to go. Be well.
Vary your exit times. Avoid the rush from hell.

Trout Sky

Of course you can't see your feet and can only feel
What your feet see, the uneven, pebbled, grassy
    Dirt, when you walk out to the lake at night to fall
In love. From the calm, you'd expect a glassy
Surface to reflect the heavens and a distant birdcall
    To surprise you with a whisper's intimacy
At least once or twice before you return to the world.

But Lilliputian waves gulliver the senses: they bully
Mirror and hearer both until your only choice
    Is to recognize their authority. They're almost silly,
As they invisibly sidle and sully, but to chase
Them away you'd have to be the moon. What is fully
    There? Only the Jeffrey pines, their chaise
Longue languor spelled out in butterscotch letters.

Near Affair

To keep our affair near,
I fixed my eyes on the trees
By the tennis courts
And other rooted
Things: apartment houses,
Street lamps, the jungle gyms
Where your children,
Like the breeze-
Responsive, younger
And frailer limbs
Of the trees, clashed.
Being adjacent may have
Substituted
For being embraced, but
That barely parted
Pair of jacarandas
Had nothing to prove.
I fell in love with those trees
And made no move.

After-Dinner Sonnet

If wonders vie in the real
World, let this qualify:
The boy has more food
On his plate *after* his meal.

When it's served to him
The fried rice, broccoli
Spears, and teriyaki slices
Are flush with the rim

Of the bowl; after plowing
Through and turning
Over the steamy feast,
The dish is overflowing.

Earthlings, mimic this mouth:
Eat up. Cultivate growth.

III

Boomerangs

Fearsome)

Fearsome
cliché: "Moderation in Everything" is bandied
immoderately, including
here.

Wuthering}

Wuthering
weather. Father, nautically a novice,
sailed from the shore
of Mother.

Hope)

Hope
or superstition? Not closing entirely
is how old warped pantry
doors cope.

New)

New cat
in a box of old cards. One of us
asks, *Who's Kait?*
Kait who?

GOD

God
left? After the breakfast
I made Her?
Odd . . .

Leave)

Leave
wrecks be; the heart will
restore them. Leave
Rex be.

Rented

Rented,
our lives are rented. Return
delighted-in, and
dented.

AVALANCHE)

Avalanche
Chutes. A run I whistled down.
Yet I can't outski Hate's
lava.

Girls)

Girls
change into prom dresses, or *in* them,
and limo doors open
for pearls.

Outrage)

Outrage
loves the conspicuous absence:
a pumpkin sage lasagna
without sage.

Wisteria)

Wisteria
bedpost: a blossom for every time
we kissed,
Maria.

Major)

Major
literary event—blowhard! Sure,
I'd read it, if I lost
a wager.

Fairness)

Fairness
fouled: a beautiful seabird
not rescued because
not rare.

LAKE)

Lake-man,
I temper, reflect, and amplify;
I pretend I'm
awake.

Speed's)

Speed's
the boat. Follow's the Skier.
Love is all the tow-rope
needs.

How)

How
to put food on the table,
the cleaver asked
the cow.

Insulted)

Insulted
the office to pay compliments outside:
surfaces glowed, souls
exulted.

JESUS)

"Jesus
Christ Is a Shill" on Broadway?
That's it. No more church
to appease us.

PREPARING

Preparing
lunches for money—the touching
simulacrum of
caring.

Cherry)

Cherry
blossoms rain and fill the branches'
reflection, plentiful and
plenipotentiary.

Rushflowers

Rushflowers—
the lovely, blowsy, grounded
camellias are suicide's
brochures.

Crow)

Crow!
Crushed under my tires.
And *now* I
slow . . .

Dawn)

Dawn Camellia,
Sweetness Orange, Waving Arm
of the Maple, and Love
Gone.

WERE)

Were you
mine? Faded birds in
the bindweed
stir . . .